One top dog

Written by Bronwyn Tainui
Illustrated by Fabiano Fiorin

raintree
a Capstone company — publishers for children

Nick has lots of fun at Pop's. Pop is Nick's mum's dad. Pop has a dog, Ruff.

"Pop! Ruff!"

"Bow wow!"

"It's good to see you, Nick! Look at this."

"Ruff is a top dog. He can go to this."

"Ruff **is** a top dog, but he sits a lot. Dogs need to run to do that."

They all go to the park to get Ruff fit. Ruff sits and looks.

"Get it, Ruff. Good dog!"

"Go on, Ruff. You can do it!"

"Woof!"

Ruff sits and sits. Pop lets out a sigh.

"Dear old Ruff. He cannot run."

"Ruff is not too old, Pop. He will run, if we run, too."

Pop and Nick run. Ruff looks at them.

"Ruff, run! Quick! Good dog, Ruff!"

"Bow wow."

"You can do it, Ruff."

Then they meet a big dog.

"Woof! Woof!"

"That's a big dog! He might fight me and I might get hurt."

Then Pop sets this up for Ruff to go in. Ruff sits. He will not go in.

Go in, Ruff. Good dog!

Get in, Ruff. You can do it.

No! Ruff will not do it!

Nick, I think you will have to go in.

Me?

Yes. If you go in, Ruff might go in, as well.

So, Nick gets in.

Go on, Nick. You can do it.

It is a tight fit, Pop.

Oh yum!

Then Ruff gets in.

Get in, Ruff.

I'm in, Nick.

Go on, Ruff. Good dog!

It is dark in there.

I need a light.

Nick?

Good dog, Ruff. You can do it, pal!

Nick and Ruff are in.

There they are! All for me!

We are in. Now, how do we get out?

Oh dear! Oh dear! Oh dear!

Good luck, Ruff. I think you will need it.

They are fit!

It is Ruff and Pop's turn, now. Off they go.

Go in and out, Ruff. Zigzag!

No! I will not go in and out. You zigzag for me.

Pop is down. Ruff is down, too.

Oh no! No! No!

Pop gets up.

I am good. Let's go!

Do we have to?

Pop and Ruff run on.

Good luck!

Go in, Ruff. Good dog!

No! I will not go in.

You can do it, Ruff.

Pop is going in. Ruff sits and looks.

Oh no! Do not go in there, Pop!

Pop's legs kick in the air.

Oh dear!

Oh no! Look at that man. This is not good. This is bad!

"Yank me out. Quick!"

"Oh dear, Pop! This looks bad."

Ruff licks Pop.

"Oh well! Too bad!"

"Top man, Pop!"

"You have finished!"

Pop and Ruff run a lap.

Top job!

Good dog, Ruff.

Go, Pop!

Go!

Yes!

You did well!

But Ruff is in the mud now.

Get out of that muck. You have mud on your fur now.

Mud!

Then, this happens. And no one tells Ruff he is a good dog.